Dream Big

Lean In

Christian Wives

in a Divorce Culture

Shelly Hansen

S. HANSEN

ISBN-10: 0-9987186-0-2
ISBN-13: 978-0-9987186-0-6

I was able to read your book and I think it is a great topic and a great resource for someone going through this type of issue. I see quite a few people who struggle with the issues you talk about in your book and its good hear a perspective that transcends the "quick to divorce culture" we live in and see relationship struggles as an opportunity for growth and the Holy Spirits sanctifying work within the life of a believer. I think your comments on abuse were well balanced as you recommended that a person seek counsel and professional help as needed. In more complicated cases of domestic violence this is vitally important as many women excuse abuse or minimize it. If there is a danger component to the relationship, obviously they need to separate for safety. Thank you for letting me read your book. I pray God uses it to help many women.

Kind Regards,
Brian Clemmons, M.A. Licensed Mental Health Counselor
May, 2017

Shelly, thanks for the copy of your book. I read it and loved it. May the Lord use it in the lives of others to guide and bless them!

Dave Bechtel, Senior Pastor Bethel Church, Richland, WA
April 2017

DEDICATION

To my husband, sweetheart and best friend, Paul.

CONTENTS

ACKNOWLEDGMENTS

In gratitude for my mother-in-law, Jeanie Hansen,
and sisters-in-law Beth Hampton, Paulette Hansen and Shelly Kurtz.
Thank you so much for the love, friendship, prayers, conversation and mutual
support in our journey as women, wives and mothers!

You Deserve It!

Do you love watching those HGTV house flipping shows? I do too! All those fantastically creative, problem solving, hard working, "this place is a major fixer-upper but has a lot of potential if you can see past the surface and imagine this wall gone, an open floor plan, a chef's kitchen and a total re-do of the en-suite..."episodes. There is something fascinating about seeing the transformation of a tired old structure into a beautifully decorated, homey space for a family to enjoy done by a team of people working together for a shared goal. At the end of the episodes the host often proclaims, "YOU DESERVE IT!" to the family or couple.

As Christian women, we might think that about our marriage and family. "I deserve it!" That familiar message of "Receive, Redeem or Reject" applies. While we do deserve to have a fulfilling Christian life, we do not deserve an easy life or to quit when it gets tough. We deserve only the good mercies and grace of God because He first loved us, He offers us the free gift of salvation and life with Him and all His abundant grace to live out a life committed to Him and His word.

If we want a beautiful house and a lasting house, we need to build it on the foundation of the Lord.

Unless the Lord builds the house, the builders labor in vain. Unless the Lord watches over the city, the guards stand watch in vain. Psalm 127:1

The wise woman builds her house, but with her own hands the foolish one tears hers down. Proverbs 14:14

The Double Divorce

This book is for women who are passionate about following Jesus, knowing and obeying his Word, and avoiding divorce. The divorce rate for Christians is very similar to the general population: between 38-60%. * Many of us know Christians who file for divorce. My parents are both Christians and my Mom divorced my Dad. I have first-hand knowledge of the cognitive and spiritual dissonance caused by professing Christians who choose divorce for the entire family. As I have worked through the issue with the Lord and my Bible, I have come to see a Double Divorce.

The first Divorce is the one where one person goes and files at the courthouse, officially filing for dissolution of the marriage. This is often accompanied by filing for alimony and perhaps child support. ly, adultery is an acceptable breach of the marriage covenant to warrant a divorce. God sees physical union as marriage and adultery as a breaking of that union. Otherwise, Christians are to stay with an unbelieving spouse until death do us part. We will look at the supports for this in a later chapter. But basically, it is a very clear decision point to actually file for divorce.

The second Divorce is the ongoing, lifestyle rejection of God's word and the standard healthy Christian response to a known sin: confess, repent, reconcile. The second part of a Christian person choosing to divorce outside of the parameters for divorce is the lack of reconciliation both with the spouse who was left, and the family who also must now live in a dysfunctional un-reconciled family dynamic. For me, this is always highlighted during the holiday season. Instead of our family celebrating together, there is a clearly uncomfortable juggling of the divorced parties that impacts the entire family and is incompatible with healthy, mature, Bible-reading, Jesus following Christian family dynamics.

*Divorce Rate in the Church – As High as the World
http://www.focusonthefamily.com/about/focusfindings/marriage/divo
rce-rate-in-the-church-as-high-as-the-world (Retrieved 2/20/17)

The Two Stages of Divorce

Here is a very succinct description of the two stages of divorce. The first is: **Hardening of your heart.** Jesus, when asked about divorce and certificates of divorce, states that the cause of divorce is a "hard heart."

> **Jesus replied, "Moses permitted you to divorce your wives because your hearts were hard. But it was not this way from the beginning. I tell you that anyone who divorces his wife, except for sexual immorality, and marries another woman commits adultery." Matthew 19:8**

How does that happen? It happens gradually as months or years of incompatible hurts cause you to fall out of love with your spouse to the point that you do not want to be with him/her anymore. Marriage has the potential for incredible intimacy and oneness and also for unbelievable hurt, rejection and profoundly disappointing pain as you realize you are not and may never by loved in the way you desperately need to be loved. A hard heart is a natural consequence of fallen people in a fallen world. One could even argue it is a self-defense mechanism and a sign of intelligence. Who wants to keep having their heart broken and abused? Who wants to suffer endlessly?

Because marriage is vulnerability on so many levels: mental, social, spiritual, financial, and physical, it is an extremely challenging situation to be "at the mercy" of another imperfect human being. A hard heart is like scar tissue that develops on a continuously inflicted wound.

What can you do? How can you survive? Before we discuss this, let's look at the second stage of divorce.

The second stage is the breaking away from obedience to the Lord by a lack of confession, repentance and reconciliation. It is not just having a hard heart towards this one person, it is having **a hard heart towards the Holy Spirit.** I now am unwilling to listen to the Holy Spirit prompting me to look directly at the sin of divorce scripturally, recognize it as outside of God's will for a professing Christian, and take the normal steps in the ongoing cycle of Christian life to confess, repent and reconcile with others whom I have wronged.

It is interesting that in the body of Christ we are to be reconciling with one another and not living in disunity. The reality is that we have many breaches of unity within the body of Christ. Perhaps we are offended by another believer or we do something to offend another Christian in our community. We tend to just avoid, move on, changing churches and not engaging in direct reconciliation with other believers. It is easier this way and many times we don't see how reconciliation is possible. While we might avoid the humbling, unpredictable, faith work of reconciliation in the larger church body, we can't do that in our family. The blunt truth is that our family lives with an un-reconciled relationship among Christians and experiences a conflict between professed belief, clear scriptural teaching, and actions which constitute hypocrisy within the core family.

Nevertheless, God's solid foundation stands firm, sealed with this inscription: "The Lord knows those who are his," and, "Everyone who confesses the name of the Lord must turn away from wickedness." 2 Timothy 2:19

Therefore confess your sins to each other and pray for each other so that you may be healed. The prayer of a righteous

person is powerful and effective. James 5:16

Godly sorrow brings repentance that leads to salvation and leaves no regret, but worldly sorrow brings death.
2 Corinthians 7:10

Turn from evil and do good; seek peace and pursue it.
Psalm 34:14

But if the unbeliever leaves, let it be so. The brother or the sister is not bound in such circumstances; God has called us to live in peace. 1 Corinthians 7:15

Let us therefore make every effort to do what leads to peace and to mutual edification. Romans 14:19

If it is possible, as far as it depends on you, live at peace with everyone. Romans 12:18

If we confess our sins, he is faithful and just and will forgive us our sins and purify us from all unrighteousness. 1 John 1:9

Finally, brothers and sisters, rejoice! Strive for full restoration, encourage one another, be of one mind, live in peace. And the God of love and peace will be with you. 2 Corinthians 13:11

Above all, love each other deeply, because love covers over a multitude of sins. 1 Peter 4:8

Be completely humble and gentle; be patient, bearing with one another in love. Ephesians 4:2

If your brother or sister sins, go and point out their fault, just

**between the two of you. If they listen to you, you
have won them over. Matthew 18:15**

**Bear with each other and forgive one another if any of you has
a grievance against someone. Forgive as the Lord forgave you.
Colossians 3:13**

Lean in...to the Lord

Are you familiar with this new mantra? "Lean in!" Women are being exhorted not to settle for less, to fight for what they care about and stand their ground in an economy designed to support men's advancement in the corporate and academic worlds. Another great take on this concept is "Be stubborn about your goals and flexible about your methods"~ author unknown. What is a Christian woman to do with a dismal disappointing marriage? How could she possibly maintain such an outdated approach to her life as staying in a "bad" marriage? Some women may not categorize their marriages as "bad" but still struggle at times to maintain a good attitude about the challenging life-yoke of marriage.

At this point I want to reflect about what we "signed up for" when we became Christians. What exactly was our new life with Jesus going to entail? How were we going to stay faithful to the Lord through the unpredictable and at times shockingly difficult path we are on as a "disciple" of Jesus? What enticed us to commit our lives to the Lord in the first place?

The Holy Spirit

The original relationship is with the Holy Spirit. Without the work of the Holy Spirit, no one would be saved or have a desire to be saved. The Holy Spirit is our first, continuous and sustaining relationship as Christians. If you do not have a relationship with the Holy Spirit, you are not a genuine Christian. The Spirit cries "Abba Father" in the heart of the believer. The Spirit prompts the dead spirit inside of us to hunger and thirst for Righteousness. The Holy Spirit is the constant in the life of the believer. Jesus does the work of the Father and the Father sovereignly reins and directs our paths and is the source of life, love and hope. The Holy Spirit in the life of the believer is like air. Without the Spirit there is no life. A healthy believer recognizes the importance of the Spirit and draws time and again from the oxygen tank for life and sustenance.

The mind governed by the flesh is death, but the mind governed by the Spirit is life and peace. Romans 8:6

But if Christ is in you, then even though your body is subject to death because of sin, the Spirit gives life because of righteousness. And if the Spirit of him who raised Jesus from the dead is living in you, he who raised Christ from the dead will also give life to your mortal bodies because of his Spirit who lives in you. Romans 8: 10-11

Because you are his sons, God sent the Spirit of his Son into our hearts, the Spirit who calls out, *"Abba*, Father." Galatians 4:6

The Spirit of God has made me; the breath of the Almighty gives me life. Job 33:4

I signed up to be a "deny yourself and take up your cross daily", "take my yoke upon you and learn from me", "I will never leave you or forsake you", "to obey is better than sacrifice", "the joy of the Lord is my strength", "for when I am weak them am I strong" lifetime follower of Jesus. I knew this was going to be a "not by might, not by power, but by my Spirit says the Lord" kind of life. A "let your light so shine before men that they may see your good deeds and praise your Father in heaven"…"I have fought the good fight, I have kept the faith, I have finished the race" kind of walk with my Lord. Perhaps I would experience persecution for my faith, or rejection by my peers. Perhaps I would have to suffer. But life with Jesus is peace and forgiveness…grace and the promise of heaven. This clearly temporary life is a brief character and faith developing training camp in the tent of my imperfect, perishable body. I actually have the privilege of bringing God glory in my ordinary, small, but blessed life.

**He answered, "'Love the Lord your God with all your heart
and with all your soul and with all your strength
and with all your mind'; and, 'Love your neighbor as yourself.'"
Luke 10:27**

**But Samuel replied: "Does the Lord delight in burnt offerings
and sacrifices as much as in obeying the Lord?
To obey is better than sacrifice, and to heed is better than the
fat of rams. 1 Samuel 15:22**

"You are the salt of the earth. But if the salt loses its saltiness, how can it be made salty again? It is no longer good for anything, except to be thrown out and trampled underfoot.
Matthew 5:13

The Integrity of the Believer

The same principles that apply to my life as a believer apply to my marriage. The neighbor I am to love as myself includes my husband. The obeying includes obeying about marriage and divorce. The faithfulness, kindness, goodness, gentleness, self-control, forgiveness, speaking the truth in love, bearing with one another applies to my marriage and specifically to me as a wife. The bigger issue is how am I going to get through life. The answer is with Jesus. The lesser issue is how am I going to get through my marriage. The answer is the same: with Jesus. I have jotted down 8 marriage vows that I make before the Lord as a wife. These are my personal commitments as a believing wife:

1. I will apply the Gospel to my marriage. My needs are meant to be satisfied first by the Lord, not my husband. To expect my husband to fulfill all my needs negates the Gospel and puts my husband in place of God which is a form of idolatry. I will take my heart longings to the Lord first and last.

2. I will forgive. I will forgive the unforgiveable because Jesus died on the cross for those hurts. They are God's and I will leave them and trust the Lord for His justice and His sovereignty over my life.

3. I will pray for my husband, for God to bless him, bless his body, bless his heart, bless his mind. I pray God's best for my husband. I pray we will be compatible and bring God glory in our relationships with each other and others around us. I pray for his health, long life, wisdom and friendships.

4. I will be thankful for my husband, who is a gift from God to me so that I am not alone, but have a friend and a companion in life.

5. I will invest in my marriage as work unto the Lord. "Whatever you do, work at it with all your heart as unto the Lord".

6. I will guard my heart. I will guard my heart against temptation, bitterness and a lack of love. I will ask the Lord for love for my husband.

7. I will stay flexible and make adjustments. "Be stubborn about your goals and flexible about the methods."

8. I will stay in the same bed and the same home. I will move and be with my husband.

I need OUT! Where is the Grace? Cheap Grace and Costly Grace

Many of us have had an "I NEED OUT!", "driveway moment". The one where we are on the verge of a nervous breakdown or beyond clearly understanding what to do anymore. Or perhaps it happens in a quieter, dead kind of resigned way..."God's grace is going to have to cover for me because I cannot humanly do this anymore, period. I am not devoting one more minute to this person or non-existent relationship. Sometimes Jesus has to let something die, or kill something in order to save someone. He has let my marriage die and killed it to save me. I wish either he would die or I would die. This is what the meaning of grace is for me. Grace to divorce. God loves me too and I have suffered enough. My Christian family members will extend me grace and grace will cover this whole mess and make something beautiful out of a miserable situation."

That may seem extreme, but the divorce statistics amongst Christians support the reality of this kind of thinking.

Dietrich Bonhoeffer addressed cheap grace and costly grace in his book, The Cost of Discipleship. It is sourced in the entire Bible and specifically in Romans 6. Which is it? Grace to sin or Grace for the sinner? Of course it is Grace for the sinner. But what about the believer who chooses a lifestyle sin? Divorce is a very permanent lifestyle sin.

Cheap Grace

Cheap grace is like a child with a hard working parent who sacrificed to provide for the family. The child knows it is due to the grace of the parent that s/he enjoys the blessings of a stable home with a loving parent. The child takes the parent's credit card without permission and tells everyone that the card was given with permission. She starts charging on the card and purchases items the parent specifically said not to buy. When asked, the child says: "I can charge for these because of my Father's grace. He always pays for me."

While it is true, God will pay the charges for you, it is also true that this is not the intention of grace. Grace is not an account to keep drawing on, and directly disobeying His Word because God owes you Grace. The grace is to stay, do the right and difficult things in life in relationship with Him.

> "Instead of following Christ, let the Christian enjoy the consolations of his grace! This is what we mean by cheap grace, the grace which amounts to the justification of sin without the justification of the repentant sinner who departs from sin and from whom sin departs. Cheap grace is not the kind of forgiveness of sin which frees us from the toils of sin. Cheap grace is the grace we bestow upon ourselves. Cheap grace is the preaching of forgiveness without requiring repentance, baptism without church discipline, Communion without confession, absolution without personal confession. Cheap grace is grace without discipleship, grace without the cross, grace without Jesus Christ, living and incarnate." ~Dietrich Bonhoeffer

Romans chapter 6 addresses this issue head on.

Dead to Sin, Alive in Christ

6 What shall we say, then? Shall we go on sinning so that grace may increase? [2] By no means! We are those who have died to sin; how can we live in it any longer? [3] Or don't you know that all of us who were baptized into Christ Jesus were baptized into

his death? [4] We were therefore buried with him through baptism into death in order that, just as Christ was raised from the dead through the glory of the Father, we too may live a new life.

[5] For if we have been united with him in a death like his, we will certainly also be united with him in a resurrection like his. [6] For we know that our old self was crucified with him so that the body ruled by sin might be done away with, that we should no longer be slaves to sin— [7] because anyone who has died has been set free from sin.

[8] Now if we died with Christ, we believe that we will also live with him. [9] For we know that since Christ was raised from the dead, he cannot die again; death no longer has mastery over him. [10] The death he died, he died to sin once for all; but the life he lives, he lives to God.

[11] In the same way, count yourselves dead to sin but alive to God in Christ Jesus. [12] Therefore do not let sin reign in your mortal body so that you obey its evil desires. [13] Do not offer any part of yourself to sin as an instrument of wickedness, but rather offer yourselves to God as those who have been brought from death to life; and offer every part of yourself to him as an instrument of righteousness. [14] For sin shall no longer be your master, because you are not under the law, but under grace.

Slaves to Righteousness

[15] What then? Shall we sin because we are not under the law but under grace? By no means! [16] Don't you know that when you offer yourselves to someone as obedient slaves, you are slaves of the one you obey—whether you are slaves to sin, which leads to death, or to obedience, which leads to righteousness? [17] But thanks be to God that, though you used to be slaves to sin, you have come to obey from your heart the pattern of teaching that has now claimed your allegiance. [18] You have been set free from sin and have become slaves to righteousness.

[19] I am using an example from everyday life because of your human limitations. Just as you used to offer yourselves as slaves to impurity and to ever-increasing wickedness, so now offer yourselves as slaves to righteousness leading to holiness. [20] When you were slaves to sin, you were free from the control of righteousness. [21] What benefit did you reap at that time from the things you are now ashamed of? Those things result in death! [22] But now that you have been set free from sin and have become slaves of God, the benefit you reap leads to holiness, and the result is eternal life. [23] For the wages of sin is death, but the gift of God is eternal life in Christ Jesus our Lord.

Costly Grace

Costly grace is the grace of a parent with a child who continually offers forgiveness, the opportunity for restoration of broken relationship, and still maintains high standards of honesty, repentance backed by actions, and a commitment to the relationship and family. Costly grace is the beautiful fragrant oil in the family machine.

> "Such grace is costly because it calls us to follow, and it is grace because it calls us to follow Jesus Christ. It is costly because it costs a man his life, and it is grace because it gives a man the only true life. It is costly because it condemns sin, and grace because it justifies the sinner. Above all it is costly because it cost God the life of his Son.: "ye were bought at a price," and what has cost God much cannot be cheap for us. Above all, it is grace because God did not reckon his Son too dear a price to pay for our life, but delivered him up for us. Costly grace is the Incarnation of God. Costly grace confronts us as a gracious call to follow Jesus, it comes as a word of forgiveness to the broken spirit and the contrite heart. Grace is costly because it compels a man to submit to the yoke of Christ and follow him; it is grace because Jesus says: "My yoke is easy and my burden is light." The only man who has the right to say that he is justified by grace alone is the man who has left all to follow Christ. Such a man knows that the call to discipleship is a gift of grace, and that the call is inseparable from the grace. But those who try to use this grace as a dispensation from following Christ are simply deceiving themselves." ~Dietrich Bonhoeffer

Jesus encountered many people who were in a lifestyle sin. He consistently offered grace and forgiveness and the restoration of relationship . And he repeatedly exhorted: "Go now and sin no more." His grace was not and is not a celebration of sin. It is grace in the context of repentance. It is the grace found in Matthew 5's Sermon on the Mount: "Blessed are the poor in spirit, those who mourn, the meek, those who hunger and thirst for righteousness, the merciful, the pure in heart, the peacemakers, and those who are persecuted for righteousness sake."

Let not man separate

What does the Bible say about divorce? It is always important when looking at content to take two perspectives: what does this verse say and what does it mean in the context of the entire Bible. In addition, I like to look at the Old Testament, New Testament and what Jesus says to get a balanced view of instruction. What is the value being communicated? What is God's heart on this issue in light of the Gospel and His unchanging character?

Old Testament

That is why a man leaves his father and mother and is united to his wife, and they become one flesh. Genesis 2:24

"The man who hates and divorces his wife," says the LORD, the God of Israel, "does violence to the one he should protect," says the LORD Almighty. So be on your guard, and do not be unfaithful. Malachi 2:16 (NIV)

"For I hate divorce," says the Lord, the God of Israel, "and him who covers his garment with wrong," says the Lord of hosts. "So take heed to your spirit, that you do not deal

treacherously." Malachi 2:16 New American Standard Bible (NASB)

New Testament: Jesus

"Haven't you read," he replied, "that at the beginning the Creator 'made them male and female,' and said, 'For this reason a man will leave his father and mother and be united to his wife, and the two will become one flesh'? So they are no longer two, but one flesh. Therefore what God has joined together, let no one separate.

Moses permitted you to divorce your wives because your hearts were hard. But it was not this way from the beginning. I tell you that anyone who divorces his wife, except for sexual immorality, and marries another woman commits adultery."
Matthew 19: 4-6, 8

New Testament

To the married I give this command (not I, but the Lord): A wife must not separate from her husband. But if she does, she must remain unmarried or else be reconciled to her husband. And a husband must not divorce his wife. To the rest I say this (I, not the Lord): If any brother has a wife who is not a believer and she is willing to live with him, he must not divorce her. And if a woman has a husband who is not a believer and he is willing to live with her, she must not divorce him. For the unbelieving husband has been sanctified through his wife, and the unbelieving wife has been sanctified through her believing husband. Otherwise your children would be unclean, but as it is, they are holy. But if the unbeliever leaves, let it be so. The brother or the sister is not bound in such circumstances; God has called us to live in peace. How do you know, wife, whether you will save your husband? Or, how do you know, husband, whether you will save your wife? Corinthians 7:10 – 16

For example, by law a married woman is bound to her husband as long as he is alive, but if her husband dies, she is released from the law that binds her to him. Romans 7:2

Summary

- Divorce is not God's will for us. It is not his plan for a married couple
- God hates divorce and the violence it represents to the family unit
- Marriage creates one from two people
- God joins two people into one and we are not to separate/divorce. God is sovereign over our marriage.

Three Releases from Marriage

- Death of one of the spouses
- Adultery by either party
- If the other person leaves/divorces you

What about Separation?

I will share with you my perspective on separating. I think there are appropriate uses of separation. Abuse is the primary reason for separation. Abuse can be due to a variety of factors but essentially separation protects the harmed spouse (and possibly the children) from the abusive behavior. The goal of separation is reconciliation. Separation is not appropriate if the goal is not reconciliation. For example, if a woman wants to ease into the divorce by separating which provides a buffer towards full divorce, the separation is not ly motivated. The purpose of separation is to preserve the family, not undermine the family.

What about Abuse?

Abuse is real, it is miserable and it should stop. How does a Christian wife handle an abusive relationship? She handles it with all the options available to her as a faithful believing wife. God has given us resources to confront and deal with abuse. One of the tricky parts about this is that a wife is under the authority of her husband. He can inflict harm to her mentally, emotionally and spiritually in the same way parents are over their children and can abuse them as well. As Christians we see sin as a blanket issue. All people sin, all mistreatment is sin. When does sin cross over into abuse? For me the difference is that as much as you would want love to cover a multitude of sins, if it is abusive it is damaging the core of the person in a long term way. In other words, even when I extend forgiveness, because of our relationship the impact on me is a long term damage to my core self if left un-healed. Abuse takes a miracle to heal...abuse takes God to heal. Jesus dealt with sin permanently on the cross and we all live in a sinful world daily. Abuse is a sin act or acts, often over a period of time, that results in heart damage to the core of the person. Examples include incest, physical abuse, refusal within the marriage to have sex for long blocks of time, verbal outbursts of anger directed to persons, rape, controlling behaviors that are not genuinely protective - but restrictive and ongoing, drug abuse, pornography use, illegal activities, neglect and absence that is not mutually desired etc..These behaviors create a toxic marriage environment that is outside of God's will for healthy relationships. There are many ways we can abuse one another within the family and within a marriage. There are also things that are not abusive such as making poor financial decisions, growing old, not being a Christian, not exercising and being out of shape, being an incompetent father, being a teen parent, being socially inept, not getting along with your in-laws, being anti-social, having depression or mental illness, having a midlife crisis, having a long-term illness or need for care etc...

What can a Christian wife do in an abusive situation? Here are some go-to options:

- Get outside help. Reach out to your family, friends, church, and law enforcement authorities
- Go to a Christian, Bible-based counselor
- Pray, pray, pray for wisdom, discernment, strength and a miracle in your family
- As much as you can, be a Bible reading and applying person
- Give grace and maintain boundaries for a healthy relationship...not a perfect relationship but a non-abusive relationship
- Process your feelings by journaling, music, art, cleaning, exercise, loving others...you will be hurting and grieving and that is normal and part of the process through abuse to the other side
- Learn and research about the abuse issue so you are informed

- Stay committed to the marriage and seek a healthy dynamic (Be stubborn about your goals and flexible about the methods)
- Talk to your doctor or other professionals for assistance
- Choose to seek friendship and counsel from people who support you in fighting for your marriage. Be influenced by people who have the strength of character to value both you and your husband and take a long view on marriage, understanding that happiness is not the priority...doing what is right and seeking to honor God is in your better interest
- Seek to go to counseling together
- Separate if needed, and communicate a clear action needed to return to the same home situation as soon as possible
- Set a boundary...if this behavior does not stop, I need to live separately from you. I will not divorce you but I cannot live this way. If there are kids involved it may be for the safety and in consideration of the effects on the children as well. This is done in the context of an unwavering goal of reconciliation and support from others outside the marriage.

You may disagree with the above recommendations. It is absolutely a personal decision and can be scary, confusing and utterly exhausting to the point of a nervous breakdown experience. You are absolutely not alone, your marriage matters and is worth fighting for, God has not forsaken you, and there is a path for your family for healing and restoration. God absolutely does miracles and can heal hearts and relationships. He is the Reconciler.

Lord, I guess that is not for me

Long term abuse causes damage to the core of a person. A relationship that impacts you in this way, and is one of the most important relationships in your life, can result in a new psychological state. The damage impacts your psyche. Perhaps some people would say that is not possible if you are a Christian...nothing can damage you that you don't permit or allow. People are impacted by those around them and those closest to them. Sin leads to death and sometimes that death is the result of another person's actions. We all think of "you reap what you sow"...but you also reap what others, especially your immediate family members, sow. Being heartbroken requires healing. You look around and see other healthy marriages. You see happy or happier couples. You meet someone who is kind to you, seems to genuinely like you and your heart longs for that same experience in your own marriage. Your prayers include acceptance..."Lord, I guess that is not for me." I want to encourage you. While this tragedy has been allowed by the Lord in your life, it is not the final result. Stay faithful, walk through it with the Lord, and He will provide all that you need including healing your broken, damaged heart. Sin plagues us all, but God will triumph.

Not only that, but we also rejoice in our sufferings, because we know that suffering produces perseverance; perseverance, character; and character hope. And hope does not disappoint us, because God has poured out His love into our hearts through the Holy Spirit, whom He has given us. Romans 5:3-5

The Power of Submission

I want to touch on the topic of submission. ly we are to submit to one another. In the marriage, wives are to submit to their husbands, "as to the Lord." A common term for this kind of submission is complementarian. Meaning that our relationship as husband and wife is unique, it is complementary in function and the submission mandate is for final decision-making that occurs after joint discussion and consideration. If the husband wants to move, then so be it. If the husband wants to take a different job, so be it. If the husband wants the kids to go to public school or be home-schooled, so be it. Men have the final responsibility before the Lord for the family. Men are learning too and no decision is permanent and the flexibility to lead requires submission. What we don't often acknowledge is the power in submission. God gives power to the submissive. He honors the humble and He blesses the meek and obedient. It may not be evident at the time. But over time, the character of a wife who chooses to submit has a balancing value both to the marriage and family, but also personally. It develops in us a humility to knowingly submit because we are conscious of God. Do not devalue submission. It has a healthy role both in the family and in you as a person. It does not mean abdicating your role as a wife and from contributing all of your talents, thoughts, efforts into the marriage and family. Wives who take a passive, "I have no say" attitude are actually undermining the family and not submitting. They are rebelling against submitting. Stay passionate about your input, but submit to the final decisions and pray for your family and husband and watch how God works in your family for all of your good. If you have children, they will see how much you care and also how you obey God and honor your husband and love your family enough to humble yourself and submit.

Well, he isn't loving me as Christ loves the church

"Husbands, love your wives, just as Christ loved the church and gave himself up for her" Ephesians 5:25

A new angle has crept into the church's thinking about divorce. Grounds for divorce can now include violations to the "Love your wives as Christ loves the church." If my husband isn't loving me as Christ loves the church, which is what I deserve and God wants for me, then I am outside of God's will in this marriage and divorce is the solution. Our marriage falls short of God's plan. God sees my ungodly husband and loves me too much to leave me in this marriage. He isn't cherishing me like he is required to do ly, as a Christian husband. If he was loving me like God says, I would be happy and stay, but I can't stay with a man who is failing to love me as Christ loves the church."

While that may be very very true, God has not set the bar for divorce that low. Meaning that any husband who isn't loving his wife as Christ loves the church is a failure as a husband and deserves to be divorced. Only by the power of the Holy Spirit can any of us love each other as Christ loves the church "and gave himself up for her." What if that was the bar for mothering? "Mothers, love your children, just as Christ loves the church and gave himself up for them." We are flawed mothers and our husbands are flawed partners. To use this rationale is to twist the intention of the scriptures to justify our disobedience contrary to clear directives regarding marriage and divorce.

Wives in the same way submit yourselves to your own husbands so that, if any of them do not believe the word, they may be won over without words by the behavior of their wives, 1 Peter 3:1

"Happy girls are the prettiest"
The gorgeous irresistible quality of virtue

There are many kinds of beauty. Our culture puts a ton of value on outward beauty. Women who are glowing outwardly are often beautiful on the inside as well and that joy permeates their countenance. There are also women who have put a lot of effort into the externals but are not effusing genuine beauty. We want to be beautiful. Genuine beauty is inward and it shines out through your eyes and demeanor, your actions and your words. This beauty is ageless. It transcends the physical body and is the sweet and enduring result of God-honoring character and the peace that comes from a close walk with the Lord. Don't be lured to the idea that short-term "happy and pretty" equates with divorce. You will be irresistibly beautiful inside and out as your faithfulness to the Lord, commitment to your family, and long-term virtue as a person of integrity who chooses to do what is difficult for the right reasons makes you radiant.

Your beauty should not come from outward adornment, such as elaborate hairstyles and the wearing of gold jewelry or fine clothes. Rather, it should be that of your inner self, the unfading beauty of a gentle and quiet spirit, which is of great worth in God's sight. 1 Peter 3:3-4

The counselor said it was hopeless

If you are going to seek counsel, the person should have values that align with yours. A Bible-based Christian counselor can definitely be used by the Lord to support and bless you and your marriage and family. You may also have peer counselors, friends or advisors that you approach for assistance. All of those are healthy strategies for managing life-challenges. God wants us to interact with other believers for mutual support, encouragement, and wisdom. What you do not need is a person who sees your situation as hopeless. That means that God has walked away from you. He isn't in this relationship any more. Jesus, who is holding both of your hands, has dropped one and is taking one of you away in His divorce solution. There is no miracle for you, no healing, no reconciliation, no future for your family.

God is definitely still with you and there is a solution for you and your family that results in healing and restoration. God is invested in your family and isn't going to drop the ball on you. It is tempting to find a counselor who will agree with you about the impossibility of your situation and how any reasonable person would get divorced. This is not counsel. Choose a counselor who supports marriage and you both as you work through and fight for your marriage and family. Do not compromise and trade out the Bible and God for a human counselor's opinion. To later tell everyone, "the counselor said I had no other options...we had tried everything...it was beyond fixing..." is placing a counselor over God, the Bible, your commitment to the Lord and your own conscience as determining your decisions. No one will be fooled. It is an excuse that many use but no one buys because a counselor is just a counselor and you are the one who makes the decisions.

If you are going to go to counseling together, find a mutually acceptable counselor. Often a man will prefer a male counselor. Or perhaps you can find a couple to counsel you together. Pray about the counselor and stay flexible about who it is (male, female, couple) as long as the person values marriage and is not providing fully confidential sympathy, professional acknowledgement of your pain, validation of your feelings, amazement at your long endurance and profound empathy for your sad impossible situation, rubber stamps for divorces.

God gave me back my heart

I went through a challenging set of years in my own marriage. I thought my heart would not ever be the same. One day, several years later, a godly counselor said he felt like he needed to put his hands on me and pray for me. He said he didn't know why, but in the middle of a conversation he prayed for me. It was like the apostle Paul in the Bible when the scales came off his eyes. I literally got my whole heart back. All the damaged and hurt parts had been healed. The counselor had no idea, and I had not even asked God for that because I didn't think something like that could happen. It wasn't on my radar to even think to ask. I cannot tell you how fantastic it was to be a whole person again and have full "range of motion" in my heart. Several months later, my childhood friends who know me very well mentioned it when we got together...I was my "old self again" and had a happy, light heart that had been missing. It was a miracle for me and a gift straight from God.

Your kids, regardless of age, do not want a divorce as much as you do want a divorce

Remember that science precept: "Every action has an equal and opposite reaction". This applies to divorce. Kids are equally or arguably more invested in a stable home. Kids are dependents and many people seem to minimize, rationalize or discount the life-long impact of divorce on the children and grandchildren. This applies regardless of their age and whether they are living with you. Within a Christian context this is even more pronounced. If Mom and Dad believe in the God of the Bible, why aren't they able to stay married with God's help? God definitely does not want divorce for me (the child). God sovereignly put our family together and He can keep us together. That's what it means to be a Christian; you face life with God and He provides the strength and love you need to life out a life as his disciple.

Isn't that legalistic and hypocritical like a Pharisee?

Divorce is a worldly solution to a relationship challenge or challenges. In Sunday school we are taught, "There's no place you can't obey out of." Divorce by a Christian is an oxymoron. Unless the person has left you, or committed adultery, divorce undermines what it means to be a Christian. Our usual word for this is hypocrite. This tends to make people freak out. They never want to be called a hypocrite by anyone. No one but a hypocrite would ever indentify another person's behavior as hypocritical. My response to that is to look at the Bible which is full of examples and exhortations to identify sin specifically without flinching. John the Baptist was killed by Herod. What had he said or done that was so offensive? John had recognized and identified a prohibited marriage. Samuel confronted David. Jesus confronted Peter. Paul confronted the church. Peter confronted Ananias and Sapphira. Jesus confronted the woman at the well, the woman caught in adultery and the money changers in the temple. Confronting sin is actually a sign of being a believer. The goal of confronting gently and honestly is repentance of a specific sin and restoration of relationship both with God and other believers. Pastor Carlton P. Harris describes this as the immune system of the church. To be healthy we need a working, functional immune system.* A person might also see a family member who speaks out about divorce initiated by a Christian family member as being like a Pharisee. Pharisees were making comments and setting expectations for the general public. Approaching your own family member who directly impacts you is not like a Pharisee. It is like a hurt family member, whose goal is restoration of the family.

For you were once in darkness, but now you are light in the Lord. Live as children of light (for the fruit of the light consists in all goodness, righteousness and truth) and find out what pleases the Lord. Have nothing to do with the fruitless deeds of darkness, but rather expose them. Ephesians 5:8

"You are the salt of the earth. But if the salt loses its saltiness, how can it be made salty again? It is no longer good for anything, except to be thrown out and trampled underfoot. In the same way, let your light shine before others, that they may see your good deeds and glorify your Father in heaven." Matthew 5:13,16

If someone is caught in a sin, you who live by the Spirit should restore that person gently. But watch yourselves, or you also may be tempted. Galatians 6:1

How can you say to your brother, "Brother, let me take the speck out of your eye," when you yourself fail to see the plank in your own eye? You hypocrite, first take the plank out of your eye, and then you will see clearly to remove the speck from your brother's eye. Luke 6:42

"No one, sir" she said. "Then neither do I condemn you," Jesus declared. "Go now and leave your life of sin." John 8:11

Later Jesus found him at the temple and said to him, "See, you

are well again. Stop sinning or something worse may happen to you." John 5:14

*Carlton P. Harris "The Church's Immune system" November 9, 2008 http://www.cabc.org/files/recollect/rc081109_a_healthy_bodyhas_a n_immune_system.pdf (Retrieved 2/20/17)

Did you say pornography use is abuse?

I see the impact on the marriage as damaging because it takes something that belongs exclusively in the marriage relationship (sexual fulfillment) and diverts it to another. While this "other" may be a non-personal image, the impact on the shared experience of sexual intimacy is similar to adultery. The guilt and repentance process of confessing an offending sin against the other person (pornography use) is similar to how a person would respond if s/he had been cheating. I am NOT saying that someone using pornography has committed adultery and you therefore have grounds to divorce that person. Jesus did clearly emphasize that our thoughts are tantamount to the actions of murder and adultery. But the behavior of adultery is the standard. Pornography use is common and can be purposefully stopped in consideration of the marriage commitment. As a wife, you can be sensitive to this and have standards in your home for open computer use, visible computer screens in family common areas, removing printed pornography from your home including lingerie magazines etc… It is a good habit to support awareness of the ongoing temptations and remove as much as possible from your family environment. This applies to both the husband and wife.

But I tell you that anyone who looks at a woman lustfully has already committed adultery with her in his heart.
Matthew 5:26

Sex is like...

We've all heard the analogy that sex is like the fire of a marriage, you need to keep it in the fireplace and it will heat your home not burn it down. I have another way of thinking about it. It is like a gondola ride. We get into it alone and leave our bags. We go together on a short little ride that gives us a break from our normal routine. It can also give us a new perspective on our situation and relationship. Then we get out and get back to our normal life, having had a sweet private ride together.

It is essential to allow your marriage the breathing room to leave your problems, frustrations, irritations, parenting challenges, health issues, financial pressures and just be together for a little while. All those things can wait, and can actually be improved if you take the time to be together physically. Don't use sex as an issue resolver...withholding and neglecting one another until you see some results. It isn't and it isn't fair. There is no other person in the world for sexual oneness except you and your spouse. Sexual availability and involvement is part of the marriage commitment. Give sex freely to your spouse.

The wife does not have authority over her own body, but the husband. Likewise the husband does not have authority over his own body, but the wife. Do not deprive each other except perhaps by mutual consent and for a time, so that you may devote yourselves to prayer. Then come together again so that Satan will not tempt you because of your lack of self-control.
1 Corinthians 7:4-5

My divorce is my business and doesn't concern anyone else

My husband and I had a neighbor. He was in his midlife and drove around in a truck with his business advertised on the side: "Just Me Construction". He divorced his wife of over 30 years one day after they had built their retirement home together, and drove off in his rig leaving a shocked and bereft woman alone. It was a public statement of his heart: "Just me."

If this is true, you can remove large sections from your Bible. Christians are strangely tied to one another in the body of Christ. If you are a believer, your actions impact the church. Within the family, divorce impacts all of the people related to the divorce permanently. Marriages are social institutions that impact those around them and so are divorces. When a Christian divorces their partner, for other Christians it is like being in a race and your teammates are falling down, turning in their jerseys and quitting the race. Divorce is not an individual act, it is a group act. To think of your marriage as a "just me" experience is to ignore your own experience with other people's divorces. When a Christian chooses divorce, it creates a stumbling block in the body. It presents a contradictory message about who God is. God is sovereign over our lives and marriages. He does not change. He commands us to obey. He provides all that we need to manage the challenges in our lives. He gives us the Holy Spirit, our consciences, His Word and the scriptures, the church body and community and the promise of heaven. He provides grace for our weaknesses and strength for the work He has for us to do. We died to sin just as Christ died on the cross. We are baptized to symbolize this death to sin and resurrection to new life in Christ. He loved us even when we were unlovely and we are to love one another as ourselves.

A new command I give you: Love one another. As I have loved you, so you must love one another. John 13:34

Divorce creates a stumbling block for other believers in the body who see this contradiction and the stubbornly unrepentant person who still chooses to disobey God's word and also maintains a posture of being a Jesus follower, desiring fellowship in the body, (often changing churches), and forgiveness from fellow believers despite this clear disobedience and rejection of God's commands regarding marriage.

But he said to me, "My grace is sufficient for you, for my power is made perfect in weakness." Therefore I will boast all the more gladly about my weaknesses. 2 Corinthians 12:9

Therefore let us stop passing judgment on one another. Instead, make up your mind not to put any stumbling block or obstacle in the way of a brother or sister. Romans 14:13

We put no stumbling block in anyone's path so that our ministry will not be discredited. 2 Corinthians 6:3

Be careful, however, that the exercise of your rights does not become a stumbling block to the weak. 1 Corinthians 8:9

There is now a division in the body. Other believers, including those who are having marriage challenges and need the encouragement and support of other faithful Christians, will have to put in extra effort to limit interactions with the divorcing Christian who has abandoned the commitment to obeying the Lord and staying faithfully married. The divorce is, and creates, a stumbling block.

You, my brothers and sisters, were called to be free. But do not use your freedom to indulge the flesh; rather, serve one another humbly in love. Galatians 5:13

The Sweet Reward

Do you like surprises? Unexpected gifts that you weren't even imagining but that came just for you that only someone who knows and loves you could have known to give you? Those are the kinds of gifts God has for you through the course of your walk with Him and in your marriage. What those gifts are is unique to you, but also part of God's goodness to all his beloved.

Do you know an elderly woman, who has been faithful to her husband and to her Lord? What qualities does she emanate? I love hearing the stories of sweet exchanges between couples, unexpected intimacies, delights in one another, wisdom from grace upon grace, patience and long-suffering sacrificially for others out of love for the Lord and the family. The generational blessings of faith and prayer that cover over all the grandchildren and extended family.

Here are some of the surprises that God bestows. One of the unacknowledged truths about divorce is that it rejects these surprises and the God who gives them. It says: "I don't care what God can or might do, I am going my own way now. He had his chance and blew it, I choose divorce over anything God can or might do."

- **MIRACLES OF HEALING** God's answer to asked and unasked prayers for restored hearts and restored relationships.
- **HONORING OF ONE ANOTHER** Cherishing of the family and strength for the next generation when the parents have done well by staying faithful and enduring for the sake of the Gospel and one another.
- **GRATITUDE FOR STABILITY** and the security of love that covers over a multitude of sins.
- **AWARENESS OF THE POWER OF GRACE AND FORGIVENESS** in the face of continual pain and suffering in the lives of friends and the world at large.
- **SPACE FOR CREATIVITY** The freedom to use the gifts God has given you. The ability to bless others.
- **JOY FROM THE LORD** The sureness of a God who is bigger than me, bigger than my problems and is Good.

- **SEEING ANSWERED PRAYER** Watching God work through and mature us over the course of a lifetime.
- **THE OPPORTUNITY FOR INTIMACY** with God and with one another.
- **RECONCILIATION** and healing of broken hearts and relationships. Sharing of common sorrows and a depth of shared context that encompasses a lifetime of joint experiences as a family.
- **THE FACING AND BREAKING OF GENERATIONAL SINS** Those sins that are passed on from parents to children for generations may be addressed on your watch and not impact future generations in the same way.
- **THE BLESSINGS OF YOUR FATHER** who knows you, loves you, and never leaves you. He sees all your joys and pain and has your very best in His heart for you. And He has prepared heaven for you. All your hopes will be fulfilled in Him.
- **A WITNESS FOR THE LORD** A testimony of His faithfulness and goodness in your life, marriage and family. Long term marriages stand out in a world of broken families. A testimony of God's work in your marriage when your kids are working through a difficult spot in their marriages.
- **THE PEACE AND INTEGRITY** that come from obeying God's word.
- **A LEGACY OF FAITHFULNESS** for your children and grandchildren who fully know how important that is for their own futures. It can impact your child's future spouse if marrying a Christian from a solid, faithful family is a priority and s/he is seeking a stable Christian extended family to marry into.
- **THE HONOR OF YOUR CHILDREN** who see you, know you well and are grateful for you, flaws and all.
- **A HEALTHY RELATIONSHIP FOR YOUR CHILDREN WITH THEIR FATHER** It isn't popular to say "stay together for the kids' sake" but it is possible for God to work miracles in your family to the

benefit of your kids who can experience a genuine, healthy, lifetime relationship with their father supported by a solid marriage.

- **A FUN AND HAPPY FUNCTIONAL MARRIED RELATIONSHIP** You can have it too! Every relationship is unique and the dynamics between couples are one of a kind. The Lord's work in your family can bring stability, fun, and happiness that you didn't think would ever happen!

Disappointment and pain are pretty much a constant in life. But so too can be a secret walk with the Lord that can bless both you and those around you in a life well spent being light and salt in a world that needs to know about Him. Don't underestimate the miracles the Lord can and does do in families.

Her children arise and call her blessed; her husband also, and he praises her. Proverbs 31:28

His master replied, "Well done, good and faithful servant! You have been faithful with a few things; I will put you in charge of many things. Come and share your master's happiness!" Matthew 25:21

But Samuel replied; "Does the Lord delight in burnt offerings and sacrifices as much as in obeying the Lord? To obey is better than sacrifice, and to heed is better than the fat of rams." 1 Samuel 15:22

Jesus replied, "Anyone who loves me will obey my teaching. My Father will love them, and we will come to them and make our home with them." John 14:24

Who should I marry?
Marry a believer...

This may be simplistic advice, but there are two vital areas for you to consider as you approach marriage. God is clear that we are to stay married even to an unbeliever. He also sets up His plan for us to be "yoked" in the marriage relationship with believers. My husband wrote a letter to one of our children about this topic:

> *First off – I love you more than you know! I can never love you like God does, but in this world your mom and I love you more than anyone else ever has or currently does. Some day our love for you should be eclipsed by the love your husband has for you, but even his love will never even come close to how much God loves you.*
> *Your choice of a husband is by far the most important decision that you will make during the rest of your life (since you have already made the decision to trust Jesus as savior).*
>
> *I know that this feels like I am making way too much of this right now since you aren't that far down the relationship path, but you need to realize that you are now a young adult and that marriage (with or without our blessing) is an option from here on. That means that you need to decide now if you are willing to marry an unbeliever or not. If you are not, then that single issue is the first hurdle that must be passed before you go one step beyond a platonic friendship with someone. If they don't meet that minimum requirement then you shouldn't even consider allowing your*

friendship to go to the next level – it needs to be a "non-negotiable" requirement.

However, if feel that you are open to marrying an unbeliever and willing to take that chance by dating one, then please hear me out and consider the long-term consequences. We all want to believe that our faith will be strong enough to convince an unbelieving boyfriend or girlfriend to eventually become a Christian, but to go into a serious relationship and marriage that way is foolish and I don't believe that God ever asks us to take that risk. If you're not prepared to go your entire marriage and have them eventually die without ever being saved, then don't date them in the first place. Even if you're willing to risk a life with an unbelieving spouse, are you willing to put your children's salvation at risk? How about your grandchildren? Children who grow up in a home with an unbelieving father are more likely to reject Christ than to accept Him. When they have questions about death and other hard things in life, what hope does their dad have to offer if he is spiritually dead? At best he can only shrug his shoulders and say he doesn't know, but at worst he will attempt to provide some worldly explanation that only draws them further from God's truth.

Marriage is a spiritual marathon with both spouses tied to each other. It is so much harder than running the race by yourself, but when both are believers it means that one can pick the other up when they fall. To be married to an unbeliever is like running that marathon tied to a dead person. When you need them to cover you in prayer and speak words of light into your soul during a dark time, they can't...even though they will want to help and will try for a while, without the Holy Spirit in them they cannot bring spiritual truth to you.

Let me say it again – I love you so much. My heart breaks at the thought of you, your children and your grandchildren

potentially being spiritually handicapped by an unbelieving husband, father and grandfather.

*You are heavy on my mind and my heart. I will pray that God gives you wisdom, courage and comfort beyond what you can even imagine right now. I know God is working in your life every day right now and I hope you have eyes to see it so that your faith will grow strong. **This is an amazing time in life and you are an amazing young woman and one of my best friends.***

Do not be yoked together with unbelievers. For what do righteousness and wickedness have in common? Or what fellowship can light have with darkness? 2 Corinthians 6:14

...and the guy you want to be a father to your kids

There is only one man who will be the father of your child. Does this person have the character that you want for your children? He will influence and guide them; shaping their character over the developing years and into adulthood. Does he like kids? Does he like to play with them and be around children? No man is perfect and as a couple your parenting will be a joint effort that co-raises your kids. It is worth considering and praying about before marriage: Is this the man I want to father my children? Is this the husband you have for me, Lord?

Wives: Honor
Husbands: Cherish

This complementarian relationship designed by God is a simple and clear go-to perspective when you get confused and hit a rough patch in your relationship: Wives honor, Husbands cherish. If you are feeling out of sorts in your marriage it is completely appropriate to communicate the issue that is causing frustration or disharmony. Fighting, arguing, discussing, communicating are healthy. You will need to work through an infinite number of issues in your relationship over the years. We need to share our hearts honestly with each other. We need to grow in our ability to understand and accommodate one another in our marriage. While you cannot control the cherishing, you can control the honoring. Choose to honor your husband even if he doesn't deserve it. Honor him in your mind and heart and honor the Lord by wifing your husband and honoring him as your husband. Don't give up; develop a habit of being an honoring wife in private and in public and with your children. Whether his conduct is honorable is between him and God. You can still extend an honoring attitude regardless, and that is what God asks of you as a wife. It is a good posture for our hearts to stay honoring towards our husband. And it can open the way for God to work in your relationship.

Instead, speaking the truth in love, we will grow to become in every respect the mature body of him who is the head, that is, Christ. Ephesians 4:15

To wife is a verb

This has stuck with me. To wife is a verb. I first heard it when people would comment that my mother-in-law knew how to wife my father-in-law. She had become so good at wifing him that others noticed. To wife is active. It is not a passive state. It is like the other types of work God calls us to…it is effortful, it requires our time and intentional activity and it is worth doing.

Whatever you do, work at it with all your heart, as working for the Lord, not for human masters because you know that you will receive an inheritance from the Lord as your reward. It is the Lord Christ you are serving. Colossians 3:23-24

If anyone serves, they should do so with the strength God provides, so that in all things God may be praised through Jesus Christ. 1 Peter 4:11

Above all else guard your heart

If the cause of divorce is a hard heart, we need to be vigilant about guarding our heart. Marriage is similar to a marathon. It is one of the longest relationships we may have with another human being. Our culture is pro-divorce, pro-hooking up, pro-fornication, pro-living together, pro-abortion, pro-pornography, pro-starter marriages. It is around us daily. Your co-workers may extol the virtues of alimony. Your neighbor may be in a series of relationships outside of marriage. Your friend may be unwed and have several children. Your kid's friends' parents may be getting divorced all throughout their growing up years. God's word talks about putting on the armor of God. Let's put it on in our marriage. Let's put on the truth that our marriage is sacred before the Lord, the righteousness of Jesus that is by His grace, the readiness to wife in the gospel of peace, the shield of faith that God can handle me, my marriage and my family, the helmet of salvation as a believer and the sword of the Spirit which is God's word, that I've hidden in my heart that I might not sin against Him.

In practical ways, you can guard your heart. Be accountable to each other. Keep an open checkbook, open budget, open schedule, open social calendar, open computer, open television, open phone. Avoid alone time with the opposite sex. Attend functions together. Set up parameters in your life that keep you open, transparent and accountable. One of our pastors says "Marriage is like a house you build, and then...you get to live in it!" If there is a fellow you are drawn to who is not your husband, don't ignore that. Be vigilant and guard your heart against a very real temptation. Put boundaries in place that help you stay faithful to your husband. Be aware of the potential for a "work spouse." Structure your work so that it honors your husband.

Guarding our heart means taking the responsibility to choose the input we allow in our lives and staying in dialogue with the Lord so that our culture and interactions with others along with our own private thoughts, desires and contemplation are tempered by God honoring, Jesus sourced Truth.

Above all else guard your heart for it is the wellspring of life.
Proverbs 4:23

The Armor of God

Finally, be strong in the Lord and in his mighty power. Put on the full armor of God so that you can take your stand against the devil's schemes. For our struggle is not against the flesh and blood, but against the rulers, against the authorities, against the powers of this dark world and against the spiritual forces of evil in the heavenly realms. Therefore put on the full armor of

God, so that when the day of evil comes, you may be able to stand your ground, and after you have done everything, to stand. Stand firm then, with the belt of truth buckled around your waist, with the breastplate of righteousness in place, and with your feet fitted with the readiness that comes from the gospel of peace. In addition to all this, take up the shield of faith, with which you can extinguish all the flaming arrows of the evil one. Take the helmet of salvation and the sword of the Spirit, which is the word of God. Ephesians 6:10-18

Let's Chat!

1. What is your overall take on the material presented in this book? What stands out to you?

2. Do you find the concept of a double divorce scripturally accurate? Have you seen or experienced a double divorce? How has a double divorce impacted your relationship with someone? Do you see the impact in your church or community?

3. What do you think about the integrity of the believer and the intersection of marriage and wifing?

4. Dietrich Bonhoeffer was a German pastor who died in World War II in a Nazi prison. He was executed just a couple of weeks before the war ended. He was accused of being a traitor for conspiring with a group to assassinate Hitler. How does his analysis of grace match up with scripture? Do you find this challenging? Why or why not? How do you see grace in conjunction with obedience?

5. Do you feel there are broader grounds for divorce? Share an example of when you feel divorce is warranted. What scriptures support this position? Are there scriptures that advise differently? What character traits of God/the Trinity does this position represent? What character traits of God/the Trinity does this position contradict? Would you feel differently based on who initiates divorce?

6. What has been the impact of faithful marriage on you personally? What has been the impact of divorce? How has divorce impacted your children, your church and your community? Do you see any correlation between the individual decisions to divorce and cultural shifts in morality and laws in our country?

7. Respond to the statement: "My divorce is my business and doesn't affect anyone else."

8. What do you think about the section on abuse? How does that match up with or conflict with your own experiences with abuse personally or in another person's life? Have you seen an abusive dynamic resolve and result in reconciliation and a healthy relationship?

9. Intimacy requires honesty. Discuss the implications of a secret sin on marital intimacy.

10. Have you experienced a miracle in your life or marriage? What was the circumstance? Had you prayed for that miracle? What was the time frame? What was the impact on you of waiting on the Lord? How has this affected your witness?

11. What are your thoughts about going outside the marriage for help? What are the risks? Benefits? How can you maintain trust in the family and privacy for your marriage and also seek support?

12. Do you think the church supports marriages effectively? What do you think would make a difference? How has God used you to "bear another's burdens" within the body of Christ?

13. Is it possible to repent from divorce? What would that look like? Why don't more people do that within the church? Does teaching about this issue come from the pulpit?

14. Give an example of a time you were stubborn about a goal, but flexible about the methods. Have you seen that principle being applied in someone else's marriage? What did that look like? Is there an area in your marriage that you could be more flexible? What do you think would be the benefit to a more creative or innovative approach?

15. How would you respond to your child (regardless of age) who says or feels, "You would divorce me if you could." How does divorce in the family undermine trust in family member value and unconditional commitment to one another? How does it contradict the meaning of love?

16. What are primary cultural sources of temptation to divorce that impact you personally? What is one you can actively choose to avoid or set a boundary so that you are not exposed to that type of thinking? Is there a scripture that can speak truth to that lie?

17. Respond to the statement, "I will apply the Gospel to my marriage." Is it possible for God to really meet our needs for companionship, physical intimacy, and genuine love/cherishing?

18. Discuss generational sins. Do you think perhaps the reason some marriages hit challenges is because of generational sins? Why are spiritual strongholds especially difficult to address in the context of family relationships including dependent children? Have you seen victory in the area of generational sin in your own life? In your family?

19. Consider "guarding your heart" using the "full armor of God." Do you see a time frame for this or statute of limitations? Do you find this armor lacking? Have you noticed any particular part of the armor that you tend to not put on or avoid using?

20. Discuss the "Sweet Rewards" section? Are there others that weren't mentioned? Respond to the statement: "One of the unacknowledged truths is that divorce rejects these surprises and the God who gives them." What sweet rewards have you experienced in your own family and marriage?

21. Share something you think will stick with you from this material. Is there one thing you can apply to your own life and family?

Thanks for exploring this topic together!

Resources

His Needs, Her Needs by Willard F. Harley, Jr. (2002)

Love Busters by Willard F. Harley, Jr. (2002)

The Power of a Praying Wife by Stormie Omartian (1997)

Boundaries in Marriage by Cloud and Townsend (2002)

Sacred Marriage by Gary Thomas (2000)

Wild at Heart by John Eldredge (2001)

The Two Sides of Love by Gary Smalley and John Trent, Ph.D. (1992)

Created to be His Help Meet by Debi Pearl (2004)

Finding the Hero in Your Husband by Julianna Slatterly, Psy.D. (2001)

10 Things Forgiveness Is Not by Mark Driscoll (2010)
http://ekklesiamuskogee.org/10thingsforgivenessisnot/

The Cost of Discipleship by Deitrich Bonhoeffer (1937)

The Bible

All Bible references are NIV unless otherwise noted.

ABOUT THE AUTHOR

Shelly Hansen lives and works in WA state as a certified American Sign Language interpreter, teacher, mentor and author. She and her husband, Paul have been married for 29 years and have three beloved children: Erik and Kelly Hansen, Spencer and Anna Lund, and Josie Hansen. On Sunday mornings you can find her interpreting at Bethel church in Richland, WA.

Youtube: ASLInterpreter@S.Hansen

www.signotation.com

www.ingramcontent.com/pod-product-compliance
Lightning Source LLC
Chambersburg PA
CBHW060539030426
42337CB00021B/4336